PEARSON
PUBLISHING

The Student Handbook for Drama

Ideal for Key Stages 3 and 4

D1152094

Brian McG

Brian McGuire is the head of a large Expressive Arts faculty. He has a great deal of experience as a senior examiner for drama. He is recognised as one of the country's leading authorities on drama.

Illustrations created by Gary Hogg
Graphics by Matthew Foster-Smith

68665

Acknowledgement

The author is grateful to the following students for some of the example
extra   'ilson,

0068665

Name   ....

Address   ....

            ....

            ....

Exam board ....

Syllabus number ....

Candidate number ....

Centre number ....

Coursework deadlines ....

            ....

Examination dates ....

            ....

            ....

Further copies of this publication may be obtained from:

Pearson Publishing
Chesterton Mill, French's Road, Cambridge CB4 3NP
Tel 01223 350555   Fax 01223 356484

Email info@pearson.co.uk   Web site http://www.pearson.co.uk/education/

ISBN: 1 85749 521 7

Published by Pearson Publishing 1998
© Pearson Publishing 1998

Revised 1998
Reprinted twice 1999

Contents

Introduction

Drama work generally covers three areas:

- improvisational work
- rehearsed presentations
- written responses.

The purpose of this book is:

- To give you a clear understanding of the drama techniques used in improvisational drama. *Chapter 2* (pages 6 to 49) is devoted to describing these drama techniques complete with cartoon illustrations.
- To help you structure an improvisation ready for presentation. *Chapter 3* (pages 50 to 93) shows how you can develop your presentation step by step.
- To support and advise you on writing about your own drama work. *Chapter 4* (pages 94 to 115) contains many examples of written work; each example is discussed to show you why the work is effective and how it could be improved.

There are a number of forms in the book you can use to make notes. In some cases worked examples are included to show you how to use them. *Chapter 5* presents some useful information such as definitions of theatrical terms and notes on how the professional theatre is organised.

With a better knowledge of the drama techniques you use, you will become more confident with the practical side of drama and should find it easier to evaluate your work in written form.

The benefits of studying drama

Studying drama will develop skills that are important if your intention is to be involved with drama at some professional level, for example:

- performing arts courses
- acting
- stagecraft.

However, it is widely recognised that drama can also make an enormous contribution to your personal development. In today's world, employers are looking for mature, creative people who can communicate effectively – precisely the skills that drama develops.

Drama will help develop your ability to work in a team. It gives you the opportunity to understand different points of view, create your own opinions, listen purposefully and develop important language skills.

It will develop your sense of commitment and your ability to appreciate and appraise constructively.

Drama encourages planning techniques, research techniques and physical and perceptual skills.

The content of your lessons will help you understand the values, issues and culture of today's world.

In brief, it develops:

- your communication skills
- your sensitivity
- your creativity.

Of course it will also develop an appreciation of drama as an art form and its place in our society.

And it is a subject you will enjoy!

1 The drama process

In an improvisational drama project you will probably be looking at a content, particular drama techniques and some personal and social skills.

The content

This is the topic you are considering. For example, the project could be about ageism, sexism, crime, happiness or loneliness. You might meet the content through drama improvisations, or you may look at a text. A text could be:

- a script, extract or full play
- a poem or song
- a newspaper or magazine article
- letter or prose.

Often, drama teachers will use other sources for the content, for example, a painting, a photograph or an object.

As the project develops you may become aware that there are a number of issues involved. For example, *Romeo and Juliet* is the story of two lovers but the play is also about family feuding, friendship, loyalty, etc. If you are looking at a topic on loneliness you might consider the loneliness of an old person, how someone young can be lonely, how someone can be lonely in a crowd, or possible consequences of loneliness.

In the content you would consider such points as:

- what is the improvisation about?
- what lines are/or should be spoken?
- what points are being made?
- what issues are the role-plays or improvisations raising?

For example, by role-playing situations that show an old person and a young person as lonely, you may conclude that in many cases a young person's loneliness is temporary (not lasting long) and an old person's loneliness may be more permanent.

Drama skills and techniques

In order to look at the content, your drama teacher will use a variety of drama skills and techniques. For example, in a role-play you may improvise a situation with a partner, a small group or the whole class. With a partner, one of you may be the parent/guardian and the other a teenager asking for more pocket money. Role-plays can be as simple as this example but may be more complicated such as when you use the 'mantle of the expert' technique. This is where you take on the role of someone who is an expert in a particular field, for example, students in the class might be police inspectors trying to solve a crime.

There are many other drama techniques such as freeze-framing, thought in the head, prepared improvisation, script presentation, etc. *Chapter 2* offers detailed explanations of drama techniques (see pages 6 to 49). Hopefully the cartoons will help you remember the definitions.

In the drama skills you would consider:

• whether there is a freeze-frame at the beginning

• where everyone should stand in the acting area

• how certain lines should be said.

Personal and social skills

In order for the drama work to be successful, personal and social skills play an important part — skills such as concentration, organising others, making decisions, listening and planning. If you are presenting a piece of prepared drama, you need to concentrate and not drop out of role. You will have to work in a team and make decisions about the content and the way in which the presentation will take place.

You should respond to these three parts of the drama process in a creative way. Your teacher may decide that discussions or your written evaluation may concentrate on one aspect of the drama process, for example, how well you have sustained your role.

The drama process

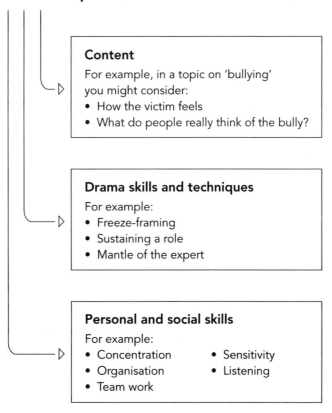

Content

For example, in a topic on 'bullying' you might consider:
• How the victim feels
• What do people really think of the bully?

Drama skills and techniques

For example:
• Freeze-framing
• Sustaining a role
• Mantle of the expert

Personal and social skills

For example:
• Concentration   • Sensitivity
• Organisation   • Listening
• Team work

When in role, or when watching the drama, you may become emotionally involved. In other words, you care about the characters and the situations. Sometimes when people watch a play they laugh, they cry or worry about the characters. This is the aesthetic, the emotional living out of the drama. This is what makes drama special — the process involves the emotions. To the content of the drama you bring your own experiences. The drama work may help you consider your point of view on the topic.

The more we examine the process of drama, the more complicated we realise it is. However, the main difference between drama and other subjects is the drama skills and techniques. A clear understanding of these will help you enjoy drama and enable you to evaluate in a constructive way.

2 Drama techniques

The drama techniques make the drama form. This is the way of presenting the drama work that you or your teacher chooses. As you become familiar with the techniques, you will be able to use them to explore or enhance your own work. The various techniques provide tools to develop ideas, character and plot. They build the drama and help you to understand the content and issues raised. It is important to have a good understanding of the techniques when writing about your drama work.

The techniques can be broken down into three areas:

- Basic role-play techniques (pages 7 to 18)
- Basic improvisation techniques (pages 19 to 30)
- Presentation skills (pages 31 to 48).

The definitions are accompanied by a cartoon to help you remember the technique.

A checklist is provided on page 49 so that you can keep a record of the techniques you have used.

Basic role-play techniques

Role-play ●

Using your own values and attitudes, you place yourself in an imagined situation.

For example, you may be a scientist on an expedition in South America. The role-play may be about the meeting of all the people who are going on the expedition. This role-play probably involves the whole group at once.

Role-plays can also take place in pairs or small groups. In pair work or small group work, your teacher may ask you to find an area in which to work. All the role-plays will begin together. An example of pair work might be one student plays the role of a parent/guardian and the other a teenager who has come home late. The beginning of the role-play is when the teenager tries to creep in the house. After the teacher's instructions, all the role-plays commence together. They finish when the teacher feels the role-plays are over.

Role-plays are not watched by an audience.

Sustaining the role ·······················

Keeping the role going, not dropping out of role.

It is sometimes difficult to concentrate on staying in role. However, the more role-plays you take part in, the easier you will find it. At first the role-plays may be short but, as you become more used to drama, the role-plays will last longer.

Preparing for the role ••••••••••••••••••••

Sometimes your drama teacher will want you to prepare for the role. *You will have to decide on background information.*

For example, when in role as an old person, you may invent family background and past events. Teachers will often use exercises to help you. For example, freeze-framing an aspect from the old person's life, hotseating or interviewing. If a lot of preparation goes on, then it is likely that your teacher will expect the role you are playing to last a reasonable amount of time. They will expect you to be able to sustain and develop the role.

Developing the role ••••••••••••••••••••••

Over a period of time and as the drama continues you build up the role.

Sometimes the role can be taken over by someone else in the group. This can give you other points of view the character might have and can also give you the opportunity to see further ideas of how the role can develop.

Language of the role ....

When in role you adopt the correct oral and body language.

Adults speak in a different way to children. Politicians have a particular way of speaking. Often getting the language right means including particular words that person would use. Think about how people greet each other. Consider the way two eleven-year-olds would greet each other. Compare this to the way two business people would greet each other: the business people would probably shake hands; the two eleven-year-olds would not. The language of the business people would probably be more formal, for example, "Good afternoon. I'm pleased to see you". The language of the two eleven-year-olds would probably be more informal, for example, "Hiya!"

Role-reversal ······································

This is where you swap roles with another student so that you can see both points of view.

For instance, one student plays the boss, the other the employee being sacked. Later in the drama they swap roles. This is often done with simple pair role-play.

Role within a role

You adopt a role in a particular situation. Your character then has to role-play some situation within the drama.

For example, if your class were playing a group of business people on a training course, you may be asked to present a mock interview. In this case you would be playing a business person playing an interviewee.

Writing in role ···································

When in role, you create written work.

This might be in the form of a letter or a diary extract. For example, as a soldier in the trench, you could complete a postcard to be sent home from the war zone. As a villager, you could complain about the proposed open-cast mine by writing a letter to the local council.

Writing in role helps you deepen your understanding of the events of the drama. A piece of writing in role can be useful to include in GCSE Drama written work. Remember that it will need some analysis or comments to go with it to place it in context within the drama.

Role-on-the-wall

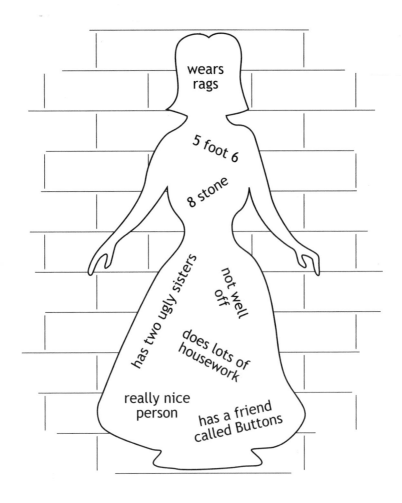

Method 1: *Your drama teacher draws an outline of a human figure on a large piece of paper, like a gingerbread man in shape. Details about the central character of the role-play are filled inside the outline by the teacher and the group.*

This builds up a picture of the central role in the drama. Information about the character's education can be written in the right arm, hobbies in the left, family background in the head and so on. Information about how others see the character or particular pressures on the character can be written outside the outline.

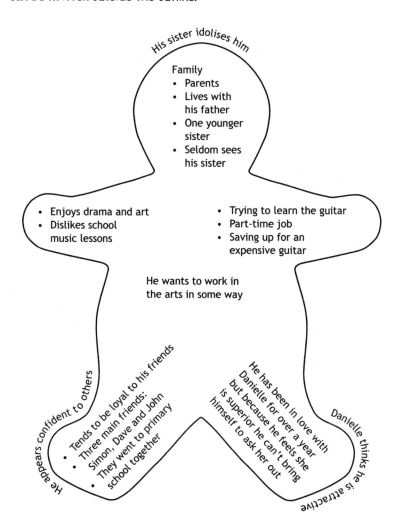

His sister idolises him

Family
• Parents
• Lives with his father
• One younger sister
• Seldom sees his sister

• Enjoys drama and art
• Dislikes school music lessons

• Trying to learn the guitar
• Part-time job
• Saving up for an expensive guitar

He wants to work in the arts in some way

He appears confident to others

Tends to be loyal to his friends:
• Three main friends: Simon, Dave and John
• They went to primary school together

He has been in love with Danielle for over a year but because he feels she is superior he can't bring himself to ask her out

Danielle thinks he is attractive

There can be a number of areas of information to write up. You can choose from the following or make up your own titles.

- Personal details
- Health
- Loves/hates
- Places of importance
- Secrets
- Recent past
- Relatives
- Intelligence
- Important items owned
- Something the person is proud of/ashamed of

- Wealth
- Job
- Ambitions
- Concerns/worries
- People admired
- Important childhood events
- Education
- Habitat

Method 2: *Each person in the role-play completes a role-on-the-wall for their role.*

This is a useful device when you are working on a prepared piece of drama, particularly for a final GCSE Drama presentation. It helps you develop credibility for your character. You can help each other with your role-on-the-wall.

Mantle of the expert

In the role-play, the group take on roles as experts.

For example, a group of detectives involved in a particular case, a group of doctors, a group of architects or designers. Generally there will be a problem that needs solving. Mantle of the expert is a popular way of involving the whole class at once. Often your teacher may give you information or ask you to complete some research about the role.

Teacher in role ······························

Here your teacher takes part in the role-play.

Your teacher could be the leader of an expedition, for example. Alternatively, they may take a less forceful role. For example, as a messenger or the assistant to the director of a company.

If you are role-playing in small groups, your teacher may join in by taking on a role. This can give the teacher the opportunity to ask questions of your role, thereby allowing you to consider issues related to the drama.

Basic improvisation techniques

Freeze-frame ······························

The creation of a still image. The action is frozen like a photograph.

Freeze-frames can focus on some part of the role-play or improvisation. At other times, the freeze-frame can be carefully built and can be the starting point for the drama. Sometimes your teacher may ask you or your group to build up the freeze-frame using one person at a time. The teacher could ask you to bring the freeze-frame to life, ie go straight into a role-play. At other times, the teacher may ask you to speak the thoughts of the character in the freeze-frame.

You may be asked to create a series of freeze-frames to give the outline of a story. When asked to do this, you should move from one frame to another with the minimum of fuss. Melting one freeze-frame into another (ie changing one freeze-frame to another in a slow, deliberate and controlled way) helps develop an awareness of space, movement and links.

When you make a freeze-frame always choose a stance you can control so that you can keep still. When you present a freeze-frame, you need to consider blocking in and you should try to make the freeze-frame visually interesting.

Spotlighting ....

During the role-play(s) the teacher asks everyone to stop apart from one person, a couple or a small group who continue with the role-play. Everyone else observes.

Your teacher may decide to start the role-play(s) again. Spotlighting could take place several times.

Focus in ··

Selecting a brief extract from one part of the role-play or improvisation.

Generally it is presented to others. The focus may only be on a freeze-frame or 15 seconds of the drama. The focus could be on a particularly important moment from the drama. For example, if the role-play is about a teenager leaving home, the focus might be 15 seconds before they walk out of the door.

Hotseating ·······································

In role and without any preparation you answer questions about yourself.

The questions can be asked by the teacher or other students. Sometimes the teacher will adopt a role and will take the hotseat. Hotseating helps build up information about a role. It helps the person in role create opinions and points of view.

Interviewing ·····························

This is where two students are in role. One of you plays the interviewee, the other the interviewer.

For example, you might play a reporter interviewing a king. In another example, the interviewer might be a doctor or a detective trying to find out particular information. There can be more than one interviewee or interviewer. This technique is a little bit like hotseating (see page 22) except all participants are in role.

Thought in the head ·

When the role-play is frozen or a freeze-frame is made, you speak the thought in the character's head.

This helps develop the role and gives you the chance to hear the thoughts of other characters in the drama. It is also known as thought tracking. Sometimes you might want to present a brief scene with the thoughts in a character's head being said by another student.

Thought tunnel ·····························

A character from the drama walks slowly between two rows of students. As the character passes each student they call out what they think the character is thinking.

For example, a person is being bullied at school. Someone takes on this role. As they walk down the thought tunnel, other students call out their thoughts:

- "I wonder what will happen today?"
- "Should I go to school?"
- "Should I report the bullying?"

For a character in a dilemma, one side of the tunnel could put one viewpoint and the other side can take the opposing view. The thought tunnel is also known as conscience alley or thought pathway.

Re-enactment ·····························

An event that you have been made aware of through the drama is re-enacted.

This is done through role-play or prepared improvisation. For example, if the drama is looking at why a person has ended up in prison then some scenes from the prisoner's childhood might be enacted.

Forum theatre ··································

Some students role-play a scene from the drama. The others in the group or class observe the role-play. The group watching can enter the scene as any character or they can stop a scene and take over a role.

For example, if the group is watching a drama about a young girl discussing her pregnancy with her mother, members of the group could join in as the father, boyfriend or sister. If you wish to take over one of the roles, you raise your hand and the teacher stops the drama by calling 'Freeze'. You then take over the role from the other player who then joins the forum (audience). When the drama is stopped, you and the rest of the group can comment or make suggestions on the characters' reactions to the dramatic situation.

How close? ●●●●●●●●●●●●●●●●●●●●●●●●●●●●●

A character from the drama stands or sits in the centre of the room. The other students take up positions of distance/closeness to that person. The distance represents the relationship between the characters.

For example, the doctor stands in the centre. Near him is the patient whose life they has just saved. Near the patient is the patient's family. Further away are the administrators of the hospital. Often in this exercise your teacher will ask for your thought in the head (see page 24).

Framing ••••••••••••••••••••••••••••••••••••••

Your teacher puts the drama into a context by helping you choose the direction in which the drama can go.

You may choose the context or issue. For example, the issue may concern a girl who is leaving home. You may show through improvisation or suggestions why the girl wants to leave home. The reasons may be different from group to group. Your teacher helps you to choose one reason. Thus the first part of the drama is framed. You may then look at incidents of the girl's life during her first week away from home. Again your teacher and the group decide on which incidents you feel are appropriate to your drama. Thus the next part of the drama is framed.

Your teacher may suggest which drama form is to be used. For example, if the drama is about villagers who are opposed to a bypass, the teacher may suggest that each of you decides on a role in the village. You might show three freeze-frames from your everyday life and one short scene of how the bypass might affect you. After these exercises, the teacher may suggest that in role you attend a meeting about the bypass at the town hall.

Caption making

You devise a phrase/sentence that suggests what the drama is about.

The caption can fit a freeze-frame or piece of drama. For example, if the drama is about an employer sacking an employee, the title might be 'No longer required'.

Presentation skills

Thinking time ····························

Time given to you before the role-play starts. You consider the information given about the role and think about how you will act in the role-play.

Fixing space ······························

You use the furniture/rostra or acknowledge boundary lines for your role-play/improvisation.

Fixing space is where you create your own functional set or space in which to work.

Improvisation/prepared improvisation · · · · · · ·

Make up and act out a storyline with little preparation. For a prepared improvisation you are given time for rehearsal.

The prepared improvisation is presented to an audience, generally the rest of the class.

Workshop presentation ····················

In workshop presentations the prepared improvisations are presented to an audience outside of the drama group.

For example, a Year 10 GCSE Drama group presents prepared improvisations on the theme of bullying to Year 7, or a Year 9 class presents work to primary school pupils on the theme of starting a new school. The workshop could include some interaction with the performance work. The visitors may be able to join in (like forum theatre) or may be given some specific follow-up tasks which may include drama work.

Mime ··

A storyline is acted out through movement and gesture without the character speaking.

Characters do not mouth words. The movement and gestures make clear the drama. Often in improvisation work there are no properties (eg glasses or cups) and so you will have to mime actions such as taking a drink or eating a meal. These situations can be difficult as you have to concentrate on your reactions to another character and the mime of holding the glass. If you forget that you are supposed to be holding a glass, this can create an unwanted comical effect.

Sequencing ·····································

In all prepared drama work there needs to be some sort of order. The storyline needs to be in a logical sequence.

You decide upon the order of events or scenes.

Voice patterns ·······························

This is how you use your voice to create the right tone for the role.

You may need to shout to show anger or whisper to show fear.
You need to consider the rhythm, pace and intonation of your
voice. For example:

- How quickly or slowly will the character speak?
- Which words would he or she stress?

Intonation is when the voice goes up or down thus adding
expression to the words.

When speaking in performance always listen to yourself. It will help slow you down and help with clarity (how clear you are).

If it sounds right to you, you are probably speaking too fast.

Remember that an audience only gets the opportunity to hear a line once. It is also important to speak with more volume than normal as your voice has to travel to reach the audience.

Addressing the audience ··················

In the presentation of a prepared improvisation, one or more of the characters speak directly to the audience.

Generally the rest of the action is frozen whilst this occurs. This allows the character to comment on events of the drama or give further information to the audience. It is a little like the role of narrator, but the person(s) addressing the audience has a role in the story.

Soliloquy

In role, you speak to the audience.

You share your thoughts, thus giving the audience further insight into your character and events.

Dramatic pause ·····························

During the dialogue a short silence is created.

A dramatic pause in the dialogue can help build up the tension. Sometimes in presentation work, the silences can be just as effective as the words spoken. Remember, however, too many silences can lose their effect.

Blocking in ·····························

This is the position someone takes in relation to the acting area and the audience.

The blocking in is to allow for sightlines, ie characters are placed on the stage/acting area so that the audience can see them clearly. When presenting improvisations, always block in the actors downstage. It makes it easier for the audience to see and hear.

The blocking in of a character can also be symbolic. For example, the king can be placed on a higher level than the servant.

Facing out of the drama ••••••••••••••••••••

In prepared improvisations, anyone from the performing group not involved with the immediate action of the drama stands and faces upstage.

With their backs to the audience, this signifies they are not involved. This helps cut down on stage traffic. Stage traffic is the movement of actors as they continually enter and exit. Facing out of the drama will help make the piece seem less disjointed and will cut down on the number of blackouts between scenes.

Slow motion ·······························

Whoa!

During part of a presented improvisation, the action is deliberately slowed. Often this is used to focus on a particular part of the improvisation.

Sometimes scenes showing such events as fights or races are shown in slow motion to give more visual impact.

Symbolism ······························

Symbolism is the use of abstract form — using gestures/ movement/words to represent the content of the drama.

When a piece is symbolic or abstract it does not look realistic. For example, if we want to symbolise pressure on teenagers we might stand one person centre stage. The other students from the group might stand on higher levels and point at the teenager. Each person may repeat one or two words to represent the pressure. One person might say 'No money', another might say 'Girlfriend', another might say 'Work', and so on. As the words are repeated, they become like a chant. The teenager eventually curls up into a ball.

Sound collage ································

Just concentrate on your driving

In sound collage, different sounds are created with voice or instruments that overlap to make a dramatic effect.

Sound collage is a useful way of creating variations in the sound the audience listens to. For example, the sounds created by the actors surrounding the man taking his driving test symbolise different sounds that may be going round his head. The repetition of the sounds will help create for the audience the confusion and stress the driver feels. The example given in the definition of symbolism also shows the use of sound collage.

In the round ·

In the drama lesson, improvisations are performed with the class sitting round the edge of the acting area.

This comes from theatre in the round, when the audience sits all around the acting area. Often the class will make a circle with their chairs.

Drama techniques checklist

You should now understand the following terms. Tick the boxes to show which ones you have used in your drama lessons:

Basic role-play techniques

☐ Role-play   ☐ Sustaining the role
☐ Preparing the role   ☐ Developing the role
☐ Language of the role   ☐ Role reversal
☐ Role within a role   ☐ Writing in role
☐ Role on the wall   ☐ Mantle of the expert
☐ Teacher in role

Basic improvisation techniques

☐ Freeze-frame   ☐ Spotlighting
☐ Focus in   ☐ Hotseating
☐ Interviewing   ☐ Thought in the head
☐ Thought tunnel   ☐ Re-enactment
☐ Forum theatre   ☐ How close?
☐ Framing   ☐ Caption making

Presentation skills

☐ Thinking time   ☐ Fixing space
☐ Improvisation   ☐ Prepared improvisation
☐ Workshop presentation   ☐ Mime
☐ Sequencing   ☐ Voice patterns
☐ Addressing the audience   ☐ Soliloquy
☐ Dramatic pause   ☐ Blocking in
☐ Facing out of the drama   ☐ Slow motion
☐ Symbolism   ☐ Sound collage
☐ In the round

3 Developing an improvisation

This chapter will help you when you prepare an improvisation for performance or an examination.

Developing an improvisation for presentation is a popular part of drama lessons. Taking an idea and developing it into a dramatic piece ready to perform for an audience gives a great deal of satisfaction. When preparing the improvisation, you need to look at how you can structure the development process. Simply repeating the play/improvisation over and over again will not necessarily improve it. There have to be ways of exploring the plot and characters so that they are credible and interesting to the audience. You need to know how to develop specific areas of performance, for example:

- vocal quality (how to use your voice)
- presenting a role (its credibility and interest)
- use of space and movement
- performance elements (pace, linking of scenes, highlights, etc).

(Pages 66 to 68 draw particular attention to these areas and consider what a drama examiner looks for.)

This chapter gives ideas for developing character and plot. For example, under the part on shaping and character development (page 56) it suggests switching roles or creating a re-enactment. These techniques help create more information about characters and could even be used as an extra scene. The methods suggested are not new. They are the tools or techniques you use during drama lessons. Normally your teacher decides what techniques will be used in a lesson, but when developing your improvisation you can choose the techniques you think will help move the drama on. These techniques are illustrated in *Chapter 2* (pages 6 to 49).

This chapter also contains tips on general performance elements such as the number of scenes, blocking, etc. There are also notes on the final rehearsals and presentation. The chapter begins with notes on selecting a theme and getting the improvisation started. There are brief references to the design work of lighting, sound and set design. However, this book does not go into detail in these areas.

As you develop a presentation, you will go through the following process:

1   **Selecting a theme** – This will be done by you or with the help of your teacher.

2   **Exploring a theme** – You will want to try out some ideas. Your teacher may create some drama lessons which allow you to explore a number of aspects of the theme before you decide on the precise nature of the improvisation. This work can often take place before groups are chosen.

3   **Choosing a group**

4   **Making sure you are aware of the examination requirements**

5   **Focus and title** – Once you focus on a theme you are going to follow, try to complete the focus boxes as soon as possible (see page 71).

6   **Initial development of context** – Once the process has begun, you need to map out a general outline of the piece.

7   **Shaping and character development**

8   **Developing the structure** – Ask yourself the following:

 • Will it keep the interest of the audience all the way through?

 • Are there particular moments of interest?

 • Are there enough/too many scenes?

9   **Developing the performance elements**, ie:

 • Voice   • Costumes/props

 • Music   • Sets

 • Lighting   • Blocking in

 • Levels

10   **Preparing and organising technical rehearsals**

11   **Preparing and organising the final rehearsal**

12   **Presenting the piece**

13   **Evaluating the piece**

Selecting a theme

Your teacher may give you a theme, or you could be asked to choose your own. There are a number of ways you can select a theme:

Topics already covered

You may like to revisit a theme completed earlier in the course or at Key Stage 3.

Topics derived from stimuli

This is a way of working often used by drama teachers. You could base an improvisation on:

- a newspaper article
- a picture or photograph
- a poem or piece of narrative
- an object
- proverbs, stories, other texts.

Often by using an object, the idea of symbolism can be introduced to the narrative. For example, a cup could belong to someone. It may be very special to them. It may symbolise a particular part of their life. When that part of their life becomes unimportant the cup is destroyed. What could the following symbolise?

- A feather
- A book
- A chair
- A pen
- A shell/conch

Text adaptations

You may wish to present extracts/interpretations from the storyline of a well-known text. Explore the theme, maybe putting the characters in different, modern or futuristic situations. How many times has *Romeo and Juliet* been interpreted? An example might be:

In 1999 Macbeth and his friend Banquo visit Blackpool. They decide to visit a fortune teller. The fortune teller makes three predictions to Macbeth.

Place

By selecting a single place for all the groups (ie a railway station, a beach) only one set is necessary.

Concepts or attitudes

Consider the themes of friendship, loyalty, trust, happiness, loneliness, honesty, justice, thoughtlessness, carelessness, time, space, influence, pressure, pride, stubbornness, sexism, racism, etc. The exploration of abstract ideas can lead into abstract drama which often gives the opportunity for good use of space and movement.

Social issues

Consider the themes of leisure, famine, poverty, crime. These themes will need back-up information. Perhaps look at one aspect or storyline.

Humanity projects

For example, the Jarrow March, open-cast mining, ecology. Look at ideas that give the opportunity to create interesting conflicts. Through whose eyes is the story told? Would it be interesting to present different points of view? It is not necessary to tell the whole story of the Jarrow March.

Specific groups

Examine the different types of characters in particular groups, for example, police, teachers, doctors. Be careful not to stereotype.

Individual stories

Devise a situation that brings a group of people together, for example, a reunion. The drama could look at extracts from each person's life.

Page 69 can be used to jot down any ideas you would like to explore.

Exploring a theme

Either your teacher will set up some exploration sessions based upon a particular theme for all students to follow or, if students have chosen different themes, use a few sessions to explore their ideas. Consider genre as a way in which the same stimulus can be presented differently. Consider comedy, mime, soap opera, documentary, dramatic rhyme, a narrator, abstract form. If the idea is not working, do not be afraid to change it.

Choosing a group

Your teacher and your group need to consider who will benefit by working together, for example:

- Will you benefit by working in a group with your friends?
- Would it be better to work in a group that has a mixture of boys and girls, or in a single sex group?
- Is everybody in the group reliable? If not, how can you encourage them to take the work seriously?

Once the themes are decided, make sure you know the examination requirements, as appropriate:

- preparation time allowed
- number of students per group
- performance time
- times and dates of final rehearsals
- times and dates of the examination.

Complete these requirements on page 70. The presentations may be performed for an examiner but you may also want to invite an audience and devise your work for a target group.

Focus and title

Early on in the process you should choose a working title for your dramatic piece. Write down the content of the piece in one sentence. This should help you choose a title. Is there a subtext? Can you write that in a sentence? For example:

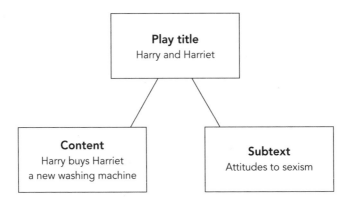

The diagram gives a focus. Filling in these boxes helps kick-start the process. It does not matter if the boxes are different at the end of the process. Use page 71 to help you.

Initial development of content

Draw up a scene synopsis (use page 73; an example is given on page 72). This will help with the direction of the piece. Once the general outline is established you can begin the shaping of the improvisation. Often the whole process is long. It is therefore important to keep motivated. As well as further discussions, the use of drama strategies/techniques will help you to shape the improvisation.

Members of your group or your teacher will suggest information and drama strategies at appropriate times. It may be possible for the teacher to suggest to all groups that they look at a particular drama technique at the same time. For example, early on in the preparation all students/groups can begin with a role-on-the-wall.

Shaping and character development

It is important to ensure that the characters you are portraying have credibility and interest for the audience. Even if the piece becomes very abstract in style, information derived from character work will be important to the development of the improvisation.

The entrance of a character is important. It establishes their role for the examiner/audience. You should think about the walk of the character, gestures that make him or her different to other characters, and ways of sharing thoughts, eg through reactions or directly addressing an audience.

The following are techniques to develop the character:
- Role-on-the-wall
- Switching roles
- Freeze-framing/thought in the head
- Hotseating/interviewing
- Creating scenes outside the drama/offstage life
- Re-enactment
- Forum theatre
- Character summary

These techniques not only help you to flesh out the character but can generate ideas for further plot development. More detail on these techniques can be found in *Chapter 2*. Further points to consider when developing a character are as follows:

Movements
- What motivates a character's movement?
- Do they move slowly when they are tired?
- How do they move when they are angry?

Gestures
Body language can indicate a person's attitude. Closed gestures, arms folded, can visually confirm 'I'm not interested'. Sometimes communication can be as simple as eye contact. Try and develop for a character particular mannerisms that set him or her apart from other characters.

Language

Accents can be difficult to imitate and can lead to stereotyping. The right register is more important than colloquialism. How a person speaks is affected by how they are feeling at that moment — nervous, happy, and so on.

During the early stages of improvisation, for example, you may find that you 'pick up' on the previous spoken line; it gives you time to think on the spot. Sometimes this creates unnecessary repetition. However, the speech patterns can be developed creatively in a positive way.

People have their own way of speaking. In these patterns they often use particular phrases. Try to personalise the character's language.

Attitude and intention

What are the character's fears, hopes, needs? These all affect movement, gesture and language. Know what the character is thinking.

Pages 74 to 83 will help you to make notes on your character:

- Pages 74 and 76 can be used to make basic notes about your character. Perhaps you could note six important facts about your character. Some example notes are given on page 75.
- Page 78 can be used to note any information you need to research. An example is given on page 77.
- Page 79 shows how you can record a character summary.
- Pages 82 and 83 are for you to make notes on the movements, gestures, language, attitude and intention of your character. If you try to explain the reactions of a character, for example, why they folds their arms, then this analysis can be useful to include in any written work that needs to accompany the practical work. Page 83 can also be used to note any changes you make to your character. An example is given on page 81.

These pages will help you to identify the development of your work when you look back over the process. Never leave the written work to the end of the practical process. Make notes and write down the changes you make as you create and rehearse the piece.

Developing the structure

Highlighting

Highlights can be used to deal with a section or the whole piece. A graph can show the frequency and degree of dramatic highlights.

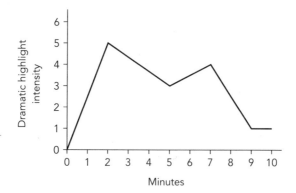

Imagine the diagram above charts a ten-minute improvisation. The first major highlight occurs after two minutes — this might be someone screaming, or running around frantically. From the second minute to the fifth minute the drama is calmer. After the fifth minute, tension begins to build up again, and falls off sharply after the seventh minute. This could be when an argument stops. Until the end of the improvisation there are no more real highlights. The drama almost seems to fade away. If all the highlights occur at the beginning and middle of a drama, or worse, only at the beginning, then the audience will lose interest. If there are no real highlights, then the piece will be lacking in dramatic tension.

Consider these structuring suggestions:

- Would a change of mood benefit the piece?
- Are you clear about the beginning, middle and end of the piece?
- Can the piece be restructured to move particular highlights?
- Can other highlights be added to the piece?
- Is there a highlight at the end of the piece?
- Are the highlights too close together?
- How could sound and light be used?
- How will the highlights link together?

Think about your improvisation. Can you draw a graph of its dramatic highlights? (Use page 84.) Seeing the highlights in graph form will tell you whether the structure of your improvisation is good, or whether it needs rethinking.

How many scenes?

Try not to present too many scenes, as this makes the storyline disjointed which works against the building of dramatic tension. Think carefully about the use of blackout between scenes/sections — they are not always necessary. Sometimes a brief freeze and then simply walking to the next position can be more effective. Consider facing out of the drama — a character or a number of characters can simply turn out of the drama and face upstage. This cuts down intrusive stage traffic. For example, at the end of a scene you could hold a freeze-frame whilst the next part of the drama continues next to or around you. Using some of these techniques will create interesting visual effects and will show a greater knowledge of performance elements.

Getting the best from your voice

To help with the pace of your piece, try the following exercises:

Picking up cues

Pick a short extract from your presentation. With a partner, go over the dialogue, overlapping cues – that is the first word of the next speaker's sentence overlaps the last word of the last speaker's sentence.

Pause

Choose another short extract of about six lines. Identify where pauses might be effective. For example, in the dialogue used below there may be a pause before the teacher's sentence, "It's possible".

Teacher: The rehearsal begins at 5 o'clock.

Student: Will it finish before six?

Teacher: It's possible.

Clarity and pace

If the pace of the dialogue sounds right in the rehearsal then you are probably talking too fast. Try and listen to yourself as you speak. It will help to slow you down. Remember that the audience only gets to hear the line once. You could record extracts and listen to the clarity and the pace.

Volume

Check out if the performance can be clearly heard. Groups can help each other in this exercise by sitting where the audience would be. Listening as a member of the audience with eyes closed really helps focus on the volume of the piece. Do the actors use the full range of their voices?

Sound collage

Sound collage is a useful technique to give another dimension to part of the drama. Using voice overlap can build up tension, create pace and develop the drama into an abstract form. It adds interest to the drama and shows awareness of performance elements.

You may wish to make notes on page 86 on the results of these exercises. An example is given on page 85.

Costumes/key props

The use of costumes and props will help create the right mood and can confirm the time the improvisation is set in. However, you do not want to be involved in numerous costume changes in a 20-minute improvisation. Consider the use of token costumes, eg using different hats, or something as simple as a scarf.

Any props you use should be really vital to the drama. If you are creating an improvisation, it is the characters and the plot that are important. If the improvisation is for an examination, then most examining boards have separate categories for design of costumes and props. In brief, keep everything simple and manageable.

Setting moods and establishing place

Music

Music selected for links should be reflective of past or future actions, and should underline the mood of the piece. If the presentation is only one short act then music at the beginning and ending helps set off the piece. Remember that the music should not impose too much. There should not be large sections of music with no drama taking place.

Sets

Very simplistic sets can often be as effective as elaborate ones. Simple colour backgrounds can give a unifying feel to a set of presentations. The colour(s) can also be symbolic of place or mood. For example, yellow for a beach, happiness or sunshine. Often the use of rostra and close lighting can be all that is needed.

Lights

Again simplicity should be the principal consideration. The angles and intensity create different effects and, of course, the coloured gels will symbolise mood. However, remember that an examiner and the audience need to see. It is better to have too much light than not enough.

Design work

In any design work that accompanies your piece, you need to consider and make notes on the following:

- The atmosphere, meaning and style the drama will convey. How can you contribute to this? For example, if it is set in the American Gangster era, or if it is futuristic, how could you show this? Can colour help, for example, what would blue lighting convey? How about red? Research can be very important at this stage, and careful notes should be made.

- Discuss the presentation with others in your group, and find out how they see it. Make notes of their requirements. Begin initial designs.

- Design light or sound plots, set, costumes and props in the context of the demands of the piece. Share the ideas with each other and note any comments. Make particularly sure that everything will be where it needs to be, and nothing will be in anyone's way. Record changes and developments.

- Construct the set/make costumes/hang lights, etc. Consider and record the differences between the design and the reality. What problems did you have, and how did you solve them?

- Discuss your ideas with the other actors. Have there been many changes? Consider the original concept. Is it still appropriate, and why?

- Record final designs.

- Consider what changes you need to make during the run. Note the details.

Cue sheets for sounds and lighting are provided on pages 87 and 88.

Positions, sightlines and levels

The phrase 'blocking in' relates to the positions the actors take up in the acting area. The actors should be positioned so that they can be seen clearly by the audience. You and your teacher need to agree on the acting area and where the audience will sit. As an exercise, you could decide upon the most important or most exciting moment from your dramatic piece. Present a freeze-frame of the moment. Other students could comment briefly on the blocking. For example:

- Is the picture visually interesting?
- Are there improvements that could be made?
- Who is the most important person in the frozen picture?
- Are they in the appropriate place?
- What is the picture saying?

Check the sightlines by appointing other students to sit around the room.

Different levels can be used to emphasise status as well as creating visual images. Using characters from your dramatic piece, make a freeze-frame that shows at a glance the status of the characters in relation to each other. (See the illustration of blocking in on page 43.) Try to use a variety of levels and bear in mind that status has a lot to do with how the character feels.

Space in the acting area can confirm the dramatic story visually. For example, if the piece concerns a conflict between a teenager and their family, the family could be grouped together and the teenager isolated to the left or right.

Use page 90 to make notes on positions, sightlines, levels, music, set, lights and highlights. An example is given on page 89.

Rehearsals and performance

The final rehearsals are to polish the improvisation ready for performance. In the final stages it is not wise to add any new ideas. Concentrate on sorting out any technical problems, and becoming really confident with your piece. If the piece is to be presented to an examiner, it is a good idea to try it out in front of a small audience first. Perhaps invite a Year 7 class. The more performances you get under your belt, the more confident with the piece you will become.

Technical rehearsals

The aim during a technical rehearsal is simply to go from the beginning of the whole presentation right through to the end, checking scene links, music and sound cues. The majority of the dialogue, apart from cues, is omitted. You may find it difficult to get on with any other work, since it is a case of being ready when needed. Those responsible for lights/sound and stage management should have all cue sheets prepared.

Technical rehearsals are a collective process and help to set the atmosphere of serious endeavour that will give confidence to everyone's performance. Establishing routines and responsibilities will lead to everyone having the calm competence from which artistic flair can grow.

Full rehearsal

Your aims here are:

- to go through the whole piece and hopefully get it right
- to keep going even if something does go wrong
- to check and note any details that need sorting out
- to try and get the right pace and tempo in the piece
- to consider how the audience will react (remember if an audience laughs, then you will have to hold back the next line briefly)
- to put together the ingredients of the performance — acting, lighting, sound, costumes, props, etc.

Presentation

On the day, you should check all props, costumes, lights and sound. The audience and examiner have only one opportunity to understand all the thinking and creating that has been done over a number of weeks. Special tips include:

- be ready
- speak so that the audience can hear and understand
- support one another in role, especially if mistakes are made
- it is too late to make any changes
- enjoy the performance
- organise clearing away for the next group.

Complete page 91 so that you have all the necessary information in one place. You may need to comment on the audience's reaction for your written coursework. If so, make brief notes as soon as possible on page 93 so that you don't forget. An example is given on page 92.

Preparing a dramatic piece for examination

In GCE A-level Performing Arts and all GCSE Drama courses there is the opportunity to develop a piece of drama from improvisation to a rehearsed presentation. Of course, you may have had this experience at Key Stage 3 as well.

A drama examiner looks for the following:

- spatial awareness, movement, gesture
- vocal quality, clarity, fluency, projection
- awareness of audience, awareness of performance elements, integration, communication
- control, appropriateness, conviction, credibility, support
- pace, timing
- interpretation, sustaining roles, responding.

These points can be placed under four headings:

1 Vocal quality
2 Supportive sustained role(s)
3 Use of space and movement
4 Performance elements

The tick boxes are to help you check individuals or a whole group. You can work with the people in your own group or with another group.

Vocal quality

	Yes	No
Is the language used by the character appropriate?	☐	☐
Does the language help make the role credible?	☐	☐
Can the vocals be heard?	☐	☐
Are the vocals projected well to the audience?	☐	☐
Are the vocals clear?	☐	☐
Does the speaker show a clear understanding of what is being said?	☐	☐
Is there rhythm, fluency and variation in the way the actors speak?	☐	☐

Supportive sustained role(s)

Do the roles support and help the drama?	☐	☐
Are the roles credible?	☐	☐
Are the roles an important part of the drama?	☐	☐
Are the responses to the action and dialogue believable?	☐	☐
Do the actors concentrate and stay in role?	☐	☐

Use of space and movement

Is the movement appropriate for the role?	☐	☐
Is the blocking in for sightlines correct? (Can everyone be seen when necessary?)	☐	☐
Is there any symbolic use of space, movement and gesture?	☐	☐
Is space used to create interesting visual images?	☐	☐
Do the gestures and movements make the roles better?	☐	☐
Is space and movement used with purpose and to help communicate the role to the audience?	☐	☐

Performance elements

Does the piece flow easily?	☐	☐
Is the piece disjointed in any places?	☐	☐
Are there any unnecessary blackouts or stage traffic?	☐	☐
Does the piece have purpose?	☐	☐
Does the piece communicate to an audience?	☐	☐
Are there a number of drama techniques included which help the roles and meaning?	☐	☐

If the piece has to be produced for a specific target audience, then you need to note any additional requirements. It may be aimed at a particular community or age group. For example, the piece may have to be on bullying and be of interest to Year 7 pupils.

Summary of tips for developing an improvisation for presentation

- If the idea is not working, change it. However, try to get the drama started as soon as possible.
- Make sure that all students in your group have an equal opportunity to show what they can do.
- Complete focus boxes.
- Complete a role-on-the-wall.
- Creating visual images is important (the play is not for radio).
- Think carefully about the credibility of the dialogue.
- Check sightlines carefully.
- The examiner will only see the performance once — make sure you speak clearly.
- Make a list of any props and costumes you need. Check that they are in the correct position for the performance.
- If you make a mistake during the performance, keep going — it may not be obvious to the examiner/audience.
- Make sure you understand the requirements of the examination performance.
- Make sure you know the date and time of your performance.

Themes

Ideas to explore

1 ....

....

....

2 ....

....

....

3 ....

....

....

4 ....

....

....

5 ....

....

....

6 ....

....

....

Examination requirements

Preparation time allowed

....

Number of students per group

....

Length of performance time

....

Dates and times of final rehearsals

....

....

....

Dates and times of the examination performance

....

....

....

Other notes

....

....

....

....

....

....

Focus

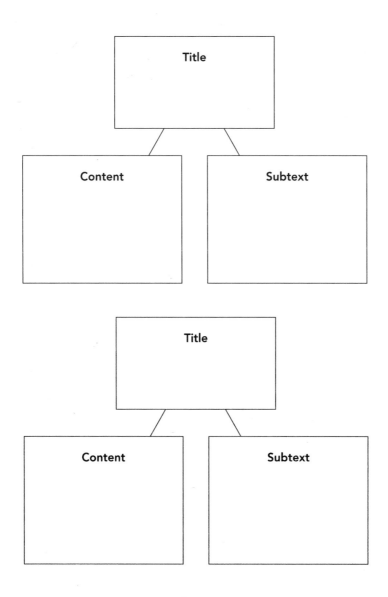

Synopsis sheet: Example

Improvisation synopsis

In the future at the age of 75 all old people are

'taken away'. Grandma's 75th birthday.

Characters

Grandma   Mary (Grandma's daughter)

Bill (Mary's husband)   Caitlin (grandchild)

Rebecca (grandchild)

Breakdown/scenes

Section 1   Family gets ready for the 'party'

Section 2   Grandma arrives

Section 3   Grandma remembers the good times

Section 4   The van arrives to take Grandma away

Section 5   The family say goodbye

Section 6   Grandma leaves

Synopsis sheet

Improvisation synopsis

....

....

Characters

....

....

....

....

Breakdown/scenes

Section 1 ....

....

Section 2 ....

....

Section 3 ....

....

Section 4 ....

....

Section 5 ....

....

Section 6 ....

....

Character description

Character notes: Example

Notes about my character(s)

1. Tom is 18 years old. He has never had a girlfriend.

2. He lives with his three sisters and mother.

3. His best friend is Sam.
   They are both interested in model railways.

4. He has done very well at school.
   He is expecting very good A-level results.

5. He has had a lot of trouble with another boy at school.
   The boy bullies Tom.

6. Tom does like Angela. She is 17 and lives round the corner.

Character notes

Notes about my character(s)

1 ....

....

....

2 ....

....

....

3 ....

....

....

4 ....

....

....

5 ....

....

....

6 ....

....

....

Character information to research: Example

Information about my character(s)

1 Some information about Tom's A-level courses
   – Geology and Spanish.

2 Names of makes of model trains.

3 Find out Spanish for "How are you?" and
   "Will you go for a walk with me?".

4 Find pictures of model trains.

5

6

Character information to research

Information about my character(s)

1 ....

....

....

2 ....

....

....

3 ....

....

....

4 ....

....

....

5 ....

....

....

6 ....

....

....

Character summary

One word or sentence that summarises my character

eg Thoughtful

....

....

....

....

One gesture that is frequently used or suggests my character

eg Rubs chin

....

....

....

....

One symbol that suggests or depicts my character

eg Arms folded moving to cupping face with hands

....

....

....

....

....

Character details: Example

Movement

I need to include some movements that suggest Tom is
nervous when speaking to Angela. In the scene when he
sits next to her, he should sit down very slowly.

Gestures

The constant rubbing of his chin with his thumb and index
finger suggests both his thoughtfulness and nervousness.

Language

He is confident when he speaks Spanish. I will have him
speaking some Spanish to Angela. There is some research to
do on certain Spanish expressions.

Attitude and intention

I need to show that he is interested in Angela in the first scene. I will make him glance across at Angela several times.

Changes I have made to my role

During the scene when Tom asks Angela out his actions were too nervous. They became comical. I have decided to make him less nervous.

Reasons for the change

I want Tom to be less nervous because I want the audience to always be on his side. When he was very nervous he became comical and the audience were laughing at him.

Character details

Movement

....

....

....

....

....

Gestures

....

....

....

....

....

Language

....

....

....

....

....

....

....

Attitude and intention

....
....
....
....
....

Changes I have made to my role

....
....
....
....
....

Reasons for the change

....
....
....
....
....
....
....

Dramatic highlights

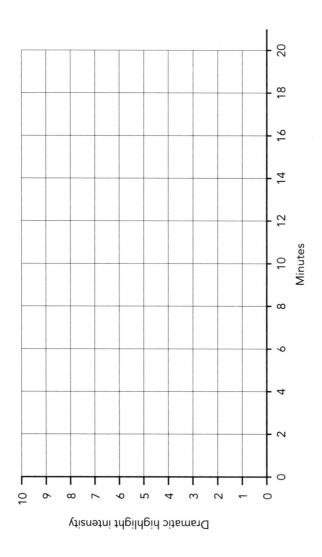

Getting the best from your voice: Example

Picking up cues

I need to rehearse the scene between Tom and his best friend. The dialogue is quite boring so we need to pick up the cues quickly.

Pause

When Tom asks Angela out, I need to pause briefly before asking.

Clarity and pace

During the bullying scene we need to speak more clearly. When Tom defends himself the dialogue here should be said quickly.

Volume

I need to speak louder during the final date scene with Angela. I have created the right tone but it is too quiet.

Sound collage

During the dream sequence we need to include a lot more different expressions. Perhaps we should try to create about ten each.

Getting the best from your voice

Picking up cues

....

....

....

Pause

....

....

....

Clarity and pace

....

....

....

Volume

....

....

....

Sound collage

....

....

....

Cue sheet: Sound

Title of improvisation

....

Cue 1: ....

....

Cue 2: ....

....

Cue 3: ....

....

Cue 4: ....

....

Cue 5: ....

....

Cue 6: ....

....

Cue 7: ....

....

Cue 8: ....

....

Cue 9: ....

....

•

Cue sheet: Lights

Title of improvisation

....

Cue 1: ....

....

Cue 2: ....

....

Cue 3: ....

....

Cue 4: ....

....

Cue 5: ....

....

Cue 6: ....

....

Cue 7: ....

....

Cue 8: ....

....

Cue 9: ....

....

Notes on dramatic piece: Example

Positions, sightlines, levels and use of space

It would be useful to create a level and leave it upstage

centre. This level can be used for the bully and Tom when he

celebrates his victory.

Music

The music used during the dream sequence is too loud.

Perhaps we should consider removing the music for this

scene.

Set

The set can be symbolic. Against the back curtain we will

hang large cut-outs of Spanish expressions, model trains and

examination papers.

Lights

We need blue lights during the dream sequence.

Highlights

The first bullying scene needs to be moved to halfway

through the improvisations. This will help with the balance of

the highlights at the beginning and end.

Notes on dramatic piece

Positions, sightlines, levels and use of space

....

....

....

....

Music

....

....

....

Set

....

....

....

Lights

....

....

....

Highlights

....

....

....

Rehearsed presentation

Title of piece

....

Specific requirements

....

....

....

....

....

Actors and roles

....

....

....

....

....

....

Equipment/costumes/props

....

....

....

Day, date and time

....

Audience reaction: Example

- Was the content appropriate for the audience?
- Do you think the audience understood the content?
- Did the audience laugh or indicate emotional involvement in any other way, eg leaning forward at tense parts, responding to audience participation opportunities?
- Did presenting to an audience make any difference to the performance?

Write your immediate comments here

During our presentation I noticed that we all spoke a lot

faster. Some of this was due to nerves I think. We all

seemed to concentrate better and picked up our cues

quickly. This meant that parts which had been slow in

rehearsal, for example, the 'snow scene', went a lot quicker.

During the scene when 'Mark' is hurt, there were a few

gasps from the audience. I think this helped us realise how

effective our drama was. This helped our confidence.

Audience reaction

- Was the content appropriate for the audience?
- Do you think the audience understood the content?
- Did the audience laugh or indicate emotional involvement in any other way, eg leaning forward at tense parts, responding to audience participation opportunities?
- Did presenting to an audience make any difference to the performance?

Write your immediate comments here

....

....

....

....

....

....

....

....

....

....

....

....

....

....

4 Producing written work

You will probably enjoy the practical side of drama, but may look upon the written work as a chore. A number of exam boards have tried to reduce the amount of written work required, however some still needs to be recorded.

Your written work celebrates your creativity. Try to regard it as a way of telling someone what you've learned through drama and what you've enjoyed about your work. The written work will help clarify your thinking about the drama process.

The written work is generally based on three aspects of the practical work:

- a series of improvisation lessons
- your development and presentation of a piece of drama
- appraisals/reviews of productions seen.

Within the development and presentation of a piece of drama, you may elect to concentrate on the technical side. For example, you may work on lighting, sound, costumes, properties, etc.

For any piece of written work at examination level, marks will be awarded for how analytical your work is — in other words, how you have evaluated the process. Note details of the drama form (the methods used) but don't just say what you did — explain why you did things in a certain way and which ways worked better.

Don't just be narrative — support the statements you make with evidence from your drama work. After each statement you write, ask yourself why or how. For example, 'I thought the drama was effective':

- Why?
- How ?
- What was happening in the drama that made it effective?

Don't be tempted to leave the written work to the end of the project. After a period of several weeks, you will have forgotten parts of the lessons. It is wise to make simple notes as a project takes place. The notes give you some sort of record and note your reaction to the work. Sometimes your opinions will change as the work progresses. Without written notes you may forget parts of the development of the drama and your own responses. You can also make notes on:

- which techniques you used
- how the techniques were used
- how effective the techniques were
- which ideas worked, which didn't, and why
- thoughts for possible ways forwards.

To note five points after each lesson takes very little time but the running record will prove very useful, for example, if you are writing up a unit of work for Key Stage 4 at the end of the project. Pages 110 can be used for keeping brief notes. You may find the example sheet on page 109 helpful.

Tips

- Title your work clearly.
  - Write down the project title, eg loyalty.
  - Note the type of drama, eg improvisation.
  - Date the work.
- Keep working notes. Make notes on the drama work as the project goes along. Don't wait until the end to write your notes.
- Don't just be narrative. Support the statements you make with evidence from the drama.
- Use the vocabulary of drama when you can.
- Note what has interested you about the drama work.
- Try to state what you have learned through the drama.
- Try to remember if there were any particularly effective moments during the project. What was so effective about them, and why?
- Are there other drama techniques you think could have been included in the project? How would you have used them?

Pages 111 and 112 can be used to keep a record of your coursework. There is a column to add grades or marks for each piece of work.

Writing about improvisation

When writing a unit of work on a series of improvisation lessons, begin by considering the content/issues raised and think about the drama skills and techniques used.

Try to write in one or two lines what the topic is about. For example:

> The topic was about stress and the different ways it affects people.

You can begin by stating what the topic is about and you could make some statement about what you have learned. For example:

> Our topic was about loyalty. It has brought to my attention the fact that being loyal does not necessarily always mean being completely honest.

You should then go on and explain how the drama work has made you draw such a conclusion.

Think about the drama skills and techniques used in the project. Possibly list them as a reference to remind you as you write up your unit. The main technique used will probably be role-play. Be aware of how any techniques used in the role-play have contributed to your understanding of the content and credibility of the drama. For example:

> In my role-play I played a pregnant teenager about to tell her mother about the situation. In the role-play I did not tell my mother straight away — I kept asking her questions about teenage pregnancy. I did this to test how she might react when I told her about my situation. To me, this seemed a realistic way of tackling the situation. As I was asking the questions I was leaving long pauses between each one. This allowed me to prepare what I was going to say next and helped build up the worries my character might be experiencing. The

pauses also created an intense atmosphere helping both of us to become involved in the situation. This piece of drama helped me realise how important silence is in creating atmosphere.

Writing about the language you or others have used in your role-play gives good evidence of your understanding of the content and the drama skills. For example:

When I was in role as a miner, some of the language I used was not appropriate. For example, the time was 1832 but when I was addressing the other miners about the owners of the mine I used a modern expression: 'We're being ripped off.'

You can discuss aspects of the body language you use in your drama, for example:

Andrew played the child. He sat slumped in the chair with his arms folded and refused to look at his parents. We decided Andrew should sit this way because we wanted to show he was unhappy.

In the next example, a student comments on how her body language changed during the role-play:

I walked over boldly to show that my character was annoyed. I wasn't feeling strong, just trying to appear so. When I confronted him my whole body language changed. At one time I even stepped back. I stuttered, I mumbled and kept repeating myself. I twiddled my fingers and kicked my feet. My partner realised he had the upper hand and acted as if he couldn't care. The role-play was spoiled when my partner pushed me as he walked away from me. I felt this was inappropriate.

Often your teacher will create situations where you will write in role. Writing in role shows how you understand the situation. It is a good idea to include extracts of your writing in role with some analysis. For example:

Dear Cath

The trenches are cold, wet and dreary. We will be going over the top in one hour. See you when I get back.

Love Bill.

This is a piece of writing I completed when we were being soldiers in the trenches. Now that I have had time to consider it, I think it is not very realistic. It is too short and lacking any emotion. If someone was going over the top, there is the chance that they may be killed. Perhaps they would write a longer and more meaningful letter.

. . . .

Diary extract:

William was taken to Durham jail last night. I will see him on Thursday. How will I pass these two days? The children have been taunted by other children in our street. Their dad's not a murderer. William is innocent but I don't believe he will be set free. They will hang him. No one has the right to do that. How strong will I be on that day? What will I do with the children? I'll have to be there. I don't want to go. I won't be able to look at him but he'll need me there. Maybe he shouldn't see me. I don't know what to do. I think, I write, I pray but there's never any sort of answer.

This is an extract from my diary when I was playing Isobella Jobling in the role-play. It was written three hours (drama time) after I was given the news that William would be hanged on Saturday. As Isobella, my minded hopped from thought to thought: thinking about William, thinking about how I would cope, and thinking about the children. I think the work is effective and shows my understanding of my role. Maybe the diary writing might have been a little more emotional.

As you create improvisation work, you will make decisions. Try to note them and, more importantly, state why you made them. For example:

We decided to put together two scenes showing a poor family and a rich family. We chose breakfast as the time for both as it showed both families in typical everyday situations and the contrast between the two could be emphasised.

. . . .

The drama needed to end with the witches vanishing. To symbolise this, we had them returning to a lower level and curling up. We also thought it was a good idea to end the drama with Macbeth on a higher level than Banquo as he had more status at that moment.

. . . .

We had the two children standing in the same position alongside each other to represent the equality that should have existed between them. We placed the teacher slightly forward of the children to show that she was in charge and was leading the children.

You can also state what might have been a better idea:

On reflection, the final freeze-frame could have been more symbolic if I had held an empty beer glass upside down. This would have indicated that money for the business had run out.

. . . .

The breakfast scene made its point, but maybe we could have created two further brief scenes to emphasise the differences between the families. Perhaps someone receiving a gift, or someone buying some clothes.

. . . .

The scene with the witches could have been improved by using slow motion as the witches curled up.

Writing about your prepared presentation

There are two main considerations here:

- The development — how the ideas have been formulated and what changes have been made to the piece throughout the rehearsals.
- The presentation — the performance.

It is probable that each time you run through either part or all of the improvisation, you will make changes or small adjustments. These need to be noted so that at the end of the project these notes can be written up into your unit of work.

With a good set of working notes you will be able to evaluate the process well and make precise references to the development of the drama.

How you use space is important and there are often changes to make here. You may make changes to the blocking. Blocking is how the actors are positioned in the acting area:

- You may make adjustments so that the actors can be seen clearly by the audience.
- You may decide that someone needs to move further up or downstage so that when someone crosses from left to right they do not have to walk round someone. Keeping the stage traffic flowing easily helps with the pace and overall effect of the piece.
- The blocking may symbolise something.

If you note this in your written work and justify your reasons this is good analytical work. For example:

> We placed John centre stage for the second scene because he was the main character of the story. We did not move John. We wanted the other characters to come to him. In a way, this showed he had some sort of power over them. As he was in the centre we could bring characters on from both sides of the stage thus avoiding any problems of people on the stage being in anyone else's way.

If the actors continually make exits and entrances this can spoil the flow of the piece. You can comment on different techniques you have used. As you justify them, this is again good analysis. For example:

> In our short piece of drama, each of us played three characters. In order to save time and too much unnecessary movement in the acting area, each time we changed character we would move upstage and face out of the drama thus indicating to the audience that the character was not in the drama. As we took on our next role, we simply turned into the drama.

. . . .

> Our brief improvisation showed the thoughts a teenager was having about his mother and father always arguing. At first, we had a brief scene with the mother and father arguing, then they would exit. Their son would enter and talk directly to the audience about the problem with his mother and father. I liked the idea of the teenager talking to the audience but we needed to make it more effective. We did this by keeping the parents on stage and getting them to hold a freeze at a particular point in their argument. The teenager entered and moving from stage left to stage right as he spoke he could point at the freeze and talk about his parents to the audience. I felt this had more impact because there was a picture there always reminding the audience of the problem. We decided that after the teenager spoke he would exit, then his parents would begin arguing again.

You will make changes to the characters you create by using drama techniques to develop the character. For example, you may use the role-on-the-wall technique to make up further information. You may use thought in the head, freeze-frame, hotseating or creating a scene that involves your character before the main drama story begins. Explain the techniques you use and how they helped you develop character. Being able to use drama terms correctly is important in the written work.

You may want to comment on how you used dialogue or voice patterns so that it could have the correct emotional impact. For example:

> When I was in role I spoke quietly and slowly to show I was worried about telling Tom I was going to leave him.

· · · · · · · ·

> In our drama I played a girl who was leaving her boyfriend. At first when we practised the scene we both did a lot of shouting. In order to give contrast to the noise of the argument, before I left I decided to whisper my last line aggressively. This created a better dramatic impact because of the contrast and it seemed to force the audience to listen carefully to what I felt was the most important line.

If your drama is more abstract in form you may analyse particular use of words. For example:

> We created a poem to explain to the audience about a baby who had been abandoned. We described the baby as 'defenceless'. We thought this word let the audience know how weak the baby was. Claire placed the baby centre stage so it would be the main focus for the audience. At the end of the poem we stood still, lifted our heads and whispered to the audience the word 'Helplessness'. We repeated it over and over, eventually fading it out. This was to symbolise that the baby could be dying. Hopefully the silence at the end of the drama left the audience wondering what was going to happen to the baby.

During the first presentation you need to consider if there is any difference between that performance and the final dress rehearsal. Note any developments that take place if the presentation is performed more than once. Consider what difference any audience makes to the performance. If it makes you more nervous, then what difference does this make to the performance? For example:

> Sarah was nervous and spoke too quickly. Unfortunately, it was difficult for the audience to understand some of her dialogue. It was evident from the conversations afterwards with members of the audience that they had missed important parts of the plot.

Audience response is important and does need to be commented on.

- Did you have the audience sitting in a particular place? Why?
- Did you make any contact with the audience during the performance? Was it sucessful? Did you manage to keep in control?
- Did the age of the audience help you decide on the content and style of performance?
- Did you pitch it right?
- Did the audience respond as you thought they would?
- Do you think the audience understood what you wanted to say?

For example:

> At the end of our play we asked the audience to tell us words that we used in the play to describe how a victim feels. They told us 12 different words. I was pleased that they seemed to understand and remember the points we were making about the victim.

. . . .

> Some of the jokes we presented were probably too babyish for Year 11. They did not laugh. In fact, in some parts a few people in the audience talked before the end of the joke. Obviously they were losing interest in the improvisation.

Writing appraisals/reviews

An appraisal/review is a response to a play or production. The writer will consider how well the play was interpreted and performed. There are a number of professional critics who write for newspapers. Plays and productions are reviewed very early in their run; often there will be preview nights when newspaper critics are invited. A poor review could mean that the production may not become popular with the general public.

Always begin your review with the details:

- name of the production
- name of company performing the production
- name of playwright
- place of performance
- date of performance.

As you write the appraisal, consider the type of company, eg professional or amateur, and the audience the performance is aimed at, eg teenagers or adults. This should affect your expectations. There is no need to note these with the details listed above as you will make reference to them in the appraisal.

It is not necessary to write a short paragraph on the storyline and background of the production unless your teacher specifically asks you.

The more productions you see and the more you write about them, the better your appraisals will become. If your course only requires you to write about one production, it is still a good idea to see as many productions as you can.

Write about the production as soon as possible. Don't leave it for a week. Write down your immediate thoughts. Maybe note:

- what you considered to be the highlight
- what you will remember about the play and why
- what you would want to change and why
- whether it kept your attention all the way through
- what you felt about the overall standard.

A five-point appraisal sheet is provided on page 114. Fill it out immediately after seeing a production. The five points need not necessarily be the same as the points mentioned on page 104. Simply note five points that strike you about the production. Use this as the basis for your appraisal. You may find the example on page 113 helpful.

You do not need to write about everything in the production. After your initial considerations, select some areas and write in detail. Always support any comment with direct references to the production seen, eg:

> I liked the performance of the actor who played Malvolio. He walked in a haughty way which suggested the personality of Malvolio. I have always felt that Malvolio does not have time for people. I did like the continual way the actor waved his right hand as if dismissing anyone he was talking to. This and many other gestures, for example, the lifting of his head when speaking to Sir Toby, contributed in creating the snobbishness of the character.

. . . .

> The fairy's side of the stage was lit very brightly. This suggested to the audience that she was angelic and pure. On the other side of the stage was the horrible Sticksaw. His side of the stage was lit with greens to suggest the evilness of his character. Sound was also used several times to create the same effect. When the fairy spoke, soft angelic music was played. When Sticksaw spoke, loud theatening music was played.

You should show that you understand the meaning of what the drama has communicated. Consider how the piece has done this. For example:

> When I watched *Oh What a Lovely War* I liked the way every time a soldier died one of the actors gave a member of the audience a poppy. The poppy symbolised the death and the giving of the poppy involved the audience in thinking about that death.

The use of symbolism is important and will often contribute greatly to the meaning of the play. It can often be seen through the costumes and lighting:

> All the good soldiers were dressed in white and the evil land owners were dressed in black.

· · · · · · · ·

> I think the director chose the colour red for the flag because red represents blood. There was a lot of red in this production to symbolise the blood. Another example was at the end of the battle when the stage was flooded with red light.

Consider exits and entrances, stage traffic and the links between scenes. These all contribute to the pace of the piece, for example:

> In *Barnum* I liked the way the actors juggled with the props and scenery for the following scene. It kept the whole production moving, it was entertaining, it was in-keeping with the circus theme, and it contributed to the overall pace of the production.

What sort of atmosphere was the director trying to create?

> The scene was supposed to be set in a lively tavern, however everyone on stage was very static and quiet. I think the scene needed some music to begin with and much more movement during the whole scene.

Look at the audience around you. How are they reacting? Where are they sat? Are the actors involving the audience in any way?

> There were five different entrances, all through the auditorium. The audience felt involved as the actors travelled through and played off them. For example, in a child's sword-fighting scene, the actors attacked the audience. This created a good fun start to the scene that later would involve a lot of audience participation.

Other things to bear in mind include:

- Was the storyline credible?
- Did this affect the style of the production in any way?
- What sort of atmosphere did the director create?
- Which parts of the production did you find the most interesting?
- Which parts did you find dull?
- Did you concentrate throughout the performance?
- If you were directing the performance, what changes would you make and why would you make them?
- What was the style of the presentation?
- What was effective or problematic with the stage traffic?
- Was the blocking in effective?
- How were the actors grouped?
- How was space used?
- Was any symbolism used?
- Did any of the performance involve the audience?
- Consider the actors' interpretations of the characters. Did you agree with them?
- Did the actors use any particular mannerisms for their characters?
- Why were the mannerisms effective/not effective?
- Was voice projection acceptable?
- Were voice patterns effective?
- How did the actors react to the other characters on stage?
- Did the actors concentrate?
- Were the actors aware of the audience?
- How did the actors use props?
- Were the links between scenes effective?
- Were any special effects used?
- How did the lights and sound contribute to the atmosphere?
- Was the production clearly lit?
- Was music used to underscore or create effects, tension, etc?
- Was the music too loud/too quiet?

- Was the music appropriate?
- Was music used to link scenes?
- Were the costumes modern?
- Did the actors use token costumes?
- What did the costumes tell you about the characters?
- Were the colours of the costumes significant?
- Were the colours of the set symbolic?
- What type of set was it?
- Was it abstract/realistic?
- How much space was used?
- Were there any special features?

Page 115 can be used to list the performances you have seen and to note brief details about them.

Notes for written work: Example

Project title   Animal rights and wrongs
....

Date   November 1998
....

1   Pair work, group work, large group work – preparing freeze-
    frames. Easier to work in small group. As groups become
    bigger, more difficult to listen and organise.

2   Freeze-frame of eight people entering a circus. Brought to
    life. Needs a loud cue to signal freeze. Used ringmaster
    saying "Hurry along".

3   Easy to block in freeze-frame but when brought to life
    many of us had our backs to the audience. It was difficult
    to keep clear blocking in with eight people.

4   Poor blocking in for final freeze-frame meant some of us
    could not be seen when we addressed the audience with
    our thoughts.

5   When we addressed the audience we could have stepped
    forward thus stepping into view.

Notes for written work

Project title   ....

Date   ....

1   ....

....

....

2   ....

....

....

3   ....

....

....

4   ....

....

....

5   ....

....

....

Key Stage 3

Work set	Deadline	Completed
....	....	....
....	....	....
....	....	....
....	....	....
....	....	....
....	....	....
....	....	....
....	....	....
....	....	....
....	....	....
....	....	....
....	....	....
....	....	....
....	....	....
....	....	....
....	....	....
....	....	....
....	....	....

Key Stage 4

Title of topic	Deadline	Mark/Grade
....	....	....
....	....	....
....	....	....
....	....	....
....	....	....
....	....	....
....	....	....
....	....	....
....	....	....
....	....	....
....	....	....
....	....	....
....	....	....
....	....	....
....	....	....
....	....	....
....	....	....
....	....	....

Appraisal immediate thoughts: Example

Name of production Bus shelter

Name of company Tynemouth Tourers

Name of playwright Kevin Wilson

Place of performance Uppington School Drama Studio

Date of performance December 1998

1 Lots of blue light used to suggest the coldness of December. Single spotlight on the abandoned baby emphasised the loneliness, etc.

2 Use of warm colours in lighting when baby reunited with her mother.

3 Speech of friend of mother not clear. Needed to speak slower.

4 The comic routine of the milkman was a welcome relief half-way through this sad story.

5 At times too much of the acting was upstage. The reunion should have been presented downstage.

Appraisal immediate thoughts

Name of production ....

Name of company ....

Name of playwright ....

Place of performance ....

Date of performance ....

1 ....

....

....

2 ....

....

....

3 ....

....

....

4 ....

....

....

5 ....

....

....

Performances seen

Title	Company	Venue	Date

5 Useful information

This chapter presents the following information in the form of definitions and lists:

- Theatrical terms
- Theatre management – explains who does what
- The acting area – explains how the four types of acting areas are set up
- The masks – explains why masks are associated with drama
- Useful words – a list of words in alphabetical order which can be used as a prompt when completing written work.

Theatrical terms

Audience: The people who watch or listen to the performance.

Auditorium: The area in which the audience sits to watch the play. In schools this can be the assembly hall, sports hall or drama studio.

Beginners: 'Beginners' is the call given to the actors by the stage manager, five minutes before the performance begins. The actors should be ready to begin.

Blackout: When the acting area is in complete darkness. A blackout can indicate the end of a scene. There is generally a blackout at the end of the performance.

Box office: The stall or area where tickets for the performance can be obtained. Schools generally do not have the luxury of a stall. For the school production the sellers may set themselves up at a particular time (often lunchtime) somewhere like the entrance hall, a classroom or drama studio.

Casting: Deciding who will play each part/role. This is generally decided by the director.

Close lighting: When the lighting concentrates on a small area. This focuses the audience's attention.

Corpsing: Laughing accidentally when in role. By coming out of role, you 'kill' the character you are playing.

Costumes: The clothes worn by the actors to help give authenticity to the character. The clothes worn give information about the character.

Cues: Signals for a response or a line from an actor. The actor's cue often comes from following the previous speaker. Those involved offstage (eg sound technicians) have cues for their actions.

Cyclorama: A large curved screen generally set across the back of the stage. Lighting effects are projected onto it to create mood and place as well as special effects.

Dress rehearsal: When the play is presented in its entirety with lights, sound and costumes. Everything is presented as it will be for the opening performance. Professional companies use this performance to make any last-minute checks on the costumes and then perform a final dress rehearsal.

Exits/entrances: When the actors come in and out of the acting area.

Flats: Frames built (often with canvas stretched across them) in order to be painted as scenery. Buildings can be painted on them or they can be painted to look like walls. Often they will have windows and doors in them.

Flying scenery: When scenery is lifted upwards or lowered. Flying scenery in and out is used in many professional productions but is generally not done for school productions.

Front of house: The area for the audience, the auditorium, entrance, refreshment areas, etc. Not the staging and backstage areas. Someone in charge of front of house would oversee publicity, box office, refreshments, usherettes and programmes.

Houselights: The ordinary lighting used in the auditorium. At the beginning of the performance the houselights gradually dim and the stage lanterns come on.

Lanterns: Special lights used to light the acting area. They help the audience see more clearly. The lanterns can be used to create atmosphere and special effects. Often the colours used will be symbolic.

Lines: The words spoken by the actors.

Make-up: Make-up helps create characters and can be useful to add a little colour to the face when the lanterns are shining on the actor. However, many drama teachers do not use it, especially if the action is very close to the audience.

Pace: How quickly or slowly the play is presented. Some scenes will be quick, other scenes might contain a number of dramatic pauses. If the whole play is presented at the same pace, it can be boring.

Performance rights: When a play is performed, the producer needs to pay the author and/or publishing company a certain amount of money. This is one of the ways in which a writer earns their living. Generally, for school productions, there are reduced rates. Box office details have to be sent to the publisher/author after the performance run. It is necessary to apply for performing rights before commencing rehearsals. The address for the rights is often printed at the front of the script.

Premiere: The first performance of a play or musical.

Properties/props: These are simple hand-held items used in the performance, for example, a glass or handkerchief. It is advisable when creating a play to remember that whatever is taken onto a set has to be taken off. Therefore it is best not to use a lot of unnecessary props. If you are involved as an actor, always check your props are in place before the performance. Take responsibility for all personal props.

Proscenium: Many school halls have the traditional proscenium arch. This is a border framing the stage. It creates the effect of 'another room' in which the actors present the performance. The audience sits end on. (See notes on *End on*, page 122.)

Rostrum/rostra: Blocks used to create different levels. Some rostra are collapsible so that they can be stored. Most schools have some sort of rostra. (Note: Rostrum – one block, rostra – more than one block.)

Script: The words written by the author(s). The script is the basis of the play.

Set/scenery: The set/scenery creates the place on the stage, for example, a palace or garden.

Sightlines: Imaginary lines running from the audience to the actors. Lines along which it should be possible to see what the director wants the audience to see.

Sound effects: Sounds created to add effects to the performance. For example, the sound of breaking glass.

Speech: An extract from the script. Words spoken by a character. Some speeches have become very famous, for example, 'Friends, Romans, countrymen, lend me your ears...'

Stage directions: Instructions about movement or particular actions the actors should make. They are often included in the script.

Stage rake: The slope of the stage. A stage can slope towards the audience. This means actors upstage can be seen by the audience.

Stage traffic: Actors' exits and entrances and movement of the actors from one place to another in the acting area.

Striking the set: Taking down the set after a performance run.

Technical rehearsal: A rehearsal where all the technical crew (lighting, sound, props, etc) can check and rehearse their cues.

Token costumes: Part costumes used to represent a character, for example, a hat or scarf. If actors are playing several characters, the use of token costumes helps the audience identify the different roles.

Trap: The trap door in the stage floor. It can be used for effective exits and entrances. By creating special lighting and sounds, it can represent another place, for example, a cave, a mineshaft or a magical well.

Understudy: Someone who learns someone else's role in case of illness. In professional companies the main roles are always understudied. This is not always possible for a school production.

Wings: The area at the sides of the stage hidden from the audience. Often actors will make their entrances from the wings. It is important to keep the wings clear to avoid accidents. Actors should stand far enough back so that the audience does not see them. Some actors will tell you that whistling in the wings brings bad luck. This comes from the times when whistling was the signal used backstage to ask for scenery to be flown in. If someone whistled at an incorrect moment, scenery appearing at the wrong time could cause an accident.

Theatre management

Actors: The performers.

Choreographer: If dance and movement are an integral part of the performance, a choreographer is the person who arranges the steps and movements. They work closely with the director.

Costume designer: The person who creates the costumes for the actors. Some of the costumes may need to be made and others may need to be bought. The costume designer often looks after the costumes during the production run.

Director: The person who interprets the script. They have a vision of what the performance will look like on stage. They spend most of their time with the actors but also coordinate stage management. The director is the driving force behind the production.

House manager: The house manager is responsible for all areas of the theatre except the stage. The house manager oversees the box office, refreshments, selling of programmes, etc.

Lighting engineer: The person who lights the set and actors. They work closely with the director creating lighting plots so that the actors can be seen easily by the audience. They also create mood and special effects as requested.

Musical director: If music is involved, the musical director interprets the music, rehearses singers, oversees band arrangements and generally conducts the band. They work very closely with the director.

Producer: The person who deals with the overall task of putting the play on. They organise the finance, performing rights, help organise publicity and oversee the buying in and hiring of materials. Often for a school production, the producer and director is the same person.

Prompter: The person who follows the script throughout the main rehearsals and during all performances. If an actor forgets their line, the prompter calls it out to them. When an actor forgets a line, they will often say the word 'Yes' to the prompter as a way of asking for help.

Property person: The person who is responsible for collecting all necessary props for the performance. During the run of the performance, they will set them out as appropriate and look after them.

Sound engineer: The person who is in charge of creating special effects through the use of sound. It may be as simple as the sound of breaking glass or it could be necessary to create numerous sounds at once. Most schools have a number of specialised CDs with sound effects on. The sound engineer will also set and check microphone levels.

Stage/set designer: The person who creates appropriate settings and backgrounds for the performance. The visual impact of their designs will indicate place and, often, mood.

Stage manager: Once the play is ready for performance, the stage manager organises the stage crew during the run of the production. Whilst the play is in preparation, the stage manager works with the director to organise the lighting and sound engineers, properties, etc.

Theatre management

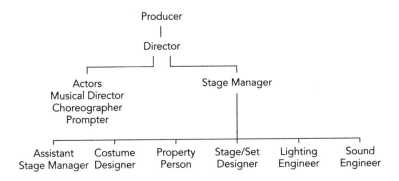

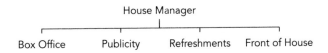

The acting area

Generally one of four types of acting area is used:

- end on
- thrust
- in the round
- promenade.

End on

The audience is directly in front of the acting. Notice in the diagram below how the stage is divided into areas. The identification of left and right is always from the actor's point of view.

Upstage right	Upstage centre	Upstage left
Downstage right	Downstage centre	Downstage left

Audience

Thrust

The audience is on three sides of the acting area.

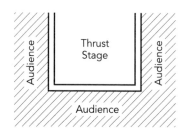

In the round (or theatre in the round)

The audience sits on all sides of the acting area:

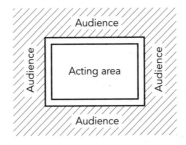

The advantage of thrust and in the round is that the actors are close to the audience so that contact is easier and the audience can see more clearly. The immediacy of these set-ups often creates a more interesting experience for the audience.

Promenade

This is when the audience follows the actors round from scene to scene. Promenade theatre is a popular method used by companies when they present drama in public parks.

The masks

The masks represent the two sides of drama: comedy and tragedy.

A comedy will have a happy ending. It will be humorous, often light and quite often satirical. A tragedy will deal with serious ideas, often disaster and death are involved.

Many plays will be both humorous and tragic in content.

Useful words

This section lists words you will find useful when completing written work. You may also wish to add words of your own.

Abstract	Action	Actor	Actress	Aesthetic
Analogy	Analysis	Appear	Appraisal	Appreciate
Appropriate	Apron	Atmosphere	Attitude	Audible
Audibility	Audience	Auditorium		
Beginning	Believable	Believe	Bias	Blocking
Caption	Centre	Character	Characterisation	Choreographer
Clarity	Confidence	Comedy	Comical	
Commitment	Communication	Concentration	Content	Control
Costume	Creative	Creativity	Credible	Credibility
Criticism	Cue	Cyclorama		
Decision	Definite	Designer	Development	Dialogue
Director	Discussion	Drama	Dramatic	
Effective	Emotion	Entrance	Evaluate	Evaluation
Exaggerate	Exaggeration	Exercise	Exit	Experience
Expert	Expression	Extract		
Form	Framing	Freeze-frame		
Gesture	Group			
Hotseat	Houselights	Humorous		
Improvisation	Inaudible	Information	Integrated	Interviewing
Issue				
Jester				
Language	Lantern	Level	Lighting	
Make-up	Mannerism	Mood	Motivate	Motivation
Movement				
Nervous				
Offstage	Organise			
Partner	Performance	Piece	Playwright	Point of view
Practical	Practice (noun)	Practise (verb)	Premiere	Prepare
Presentation	Promenade	Producer	Production	Professional
Properties	Proscenium	Purpose		
Question				
Realistic	Re-enactment	Rehearsal	Rehearse	Represent Review
Role	Role-play	Role-on-the-wall	Rostra	Rostrum
Scene	Scenery	Script	Sensitivity	Sequencing
Shakespeare	Sightline	Situation	Social	Soliloquy
Sound	Special	Spotlight	Stage	Staging
Status	Stereotype	Style	Success	Sustain
Symbol	Symbolising	Symbolism		
Teacher-in-role	Technical	Technique	Text	Theatre
Thought	Tragedy			
Understudy				
Voice				